Aldo

MALTA

Gem of the Mediterranean

Miller Distributors Limited

Miller House, Tarxien Road, Airport Way, Luqa Malta.
P. O. Box 25 Malta International Airport LQA 05
Telephone: 664488 Facsimile: 676799

Published and printed by

plurigraf

Narni - Terni
ITALIA

INDEX

MALTA

The land and the people

Lying 90 km to the south of Sicily and 290 km to the north of the African mainland, 1830 km to the east of Gibraltar and 1500 km to the west of Alexandria, Malta and its islands might be said to occupy a position in the center of the Mediterranean.

The group is composed of the islands of Malta, Gozo and Comino all of which are inhabited, and the smaller uninhabited islands of Cominotto, Filfla and St. Paul's Islands.

The total area of the archipelago is 320 km^2. The longest distance in Malta in a south-east/north-west axis is about 27 km and the widest distance is 14 km. The corresponding figures for Gozo are 14 km and 7 km. Comino, the smallest of the inhabited islands being 2.6 km^2. The length of the shoreline around Malta is 136 km and that of Gozo being 43 km. The indentations around the coast form bays, sandy beaches and rocky coves and, more importantly, deep natural harbours.

With a population of around 350,000 crowding an area of 320 km^2 the Maltese Islands can claim to be the most densely populated country in Europe.

As a result of intermarriages throughout the ages, Semitic, Latin, Rhodian-Greek and a dash of Anglo-Saxon blood has produced a rich diversity of the Maltese physical "type" and it is only where character is concerned that there is conformity. Perhaps because of his fear of being swallowed up in the crowd, the average Maltese will assert his individuality by adding his personal touch to his car, boat, house or any other of his possessions.

Prehistory

At a point of time around 4,000 BC a group of Late Stone-Age Sicilian farming families left their island home to settle in a small group of islands to the south. They brought over with them their domestic animals, pottery, bags of seeds and flint implements.

They were the first Maltese.

In time these early Maltese increased and prospered and gangs of workers could now be spared from the day to day chores so that they could give all of their time to the building of the temples.

The new immigrants were familiar with the use of copper although the tools they used were still being chipped out of flint as they had been for thousands of years.

At one time it was believed that the temple builders succumbed to an invasion of fresh migrants who exterminated, or enslaved, the original settlers and took, over the land. The invasion theory cannot be entirely ruled out and still has its adherents. If there was an invasion, the new arrivals, who, originally, hailed from the heel of Italy would have had no difficulty in overcoming the remnants of the original stock who colonized the islands some 2,200 years before.

If the first settlers were peaceful farmers (no trace of weapons of the period have been discovered) the newcomers were more belligerent. These bronze-age farmers, there is some evidence to show that they were also pastoralists, were less civilized than the folk they had supplanted, they built no temples but re-used the older, copper-age, temples as cemeteries; their dead were cremated within the walls and the ashes were deposited in the ruins of the once hallowed buildings.

The bronze-age farmers were not allowed to enjoy their islands in peace because after some 600 years of their arrival a new wave of bronze-using warriors invaded the land, and this time it was definitely an invasion, and made it their home. This event took place around 1,200 BC. Imitating their war-like predecessors, they established their settlements in easily defensible positions. The last of the three ages of antiquity — the Iron-Age — is represented in the Maltese Islands by the remains of a single settlement at Bahrija (circa 900 BC).

The Phoenicians

Their homeland a narrow coastal plain, and hemmed in by their enemies between the mountains and the Mediterranean, the only direction in which the Phoenicians could expand was seawards.

The Maltese islands with their fine natural harbours was one such outpost which the Phoenicians founded around 800 BC. As it was in other countries, so it was in Malta: having gained a foothold as traders, they gradually intermarried and integrated with the bronze-age farmers.

The larger island was now called M-L-T (Malet: meaning shelter) and the smaller island was named G-L (Gol, after the broad beamed trading vessel).

At this period of the story of Malta we are in the realm of written history, and it is recorded that overlooking the two main harbours in Malta were famous temples dedicated to Phoenician Deities — one in what is now the Grand Harbour, probably under the foundations of Fort St. Angelo, sacred to Melkart and another dedicated to Astarte in the aforementioned Tas-Silg area.

In the case of the Maltese Islands the Phoenicians did venture inland because their remains have been found in several places, even as far as Rabat in the center of the island of Malta.

The weaving industry that flourished before the arrival of the Phoenicians probably received an added boost and a wider export market. Pottery was now thrown on a wheel instead of being coiled as was previously the case.

The links between the Phoenician colonies and the Mother Country were never very strong and when the Phoenician homeland was overrun it was the Phoenician colony of Carthage that took over the rôle of Mother Country.

In many sectors of the Mediterranean littoral the Phoenician/ Carthaginians strove to establish a sphere of influence, their chief rivals in this respect being the Greeks. Surprisingly, in the Maltese Islands these differences did not seem to exist: it is not known how many Greeks lived, co-existed rather, with the Phoenicians and the Carthaginians on the Island, but some undoubtedly did — civic institutions resembled their Greek counterparts and Greek coins and pottery have been found on the islands.

The Romans

The three Punic Wars were to last for over a hundred years and during this struggle between the Carthaginians and the Romans, Sicily and its appendage, the Maltese islands, were to occupy central stage in the theatre of war for the control of the Mediterranean.

By the end of the First Punic War, in 241 BC, the whole of Sicily had been ceded to the Romans but the Carthaginians were allowed to retain the Maltese Islands.

Peace did not last long, however, because in 218 BC a second war broke out and, learning from their past mistakes, the Romans were determined to capture the islands.

Apparently the invasion did not present great difficulties and it has been suggested that the Phoenicians on the Island turned against their Carthaginian cousins and handed over the garrison to the invading Romans. The Maltese were treated more like allies than as a conquered people which lends some substance to the "collaboration" theory. The Maltese kept their Punic traditions and language and their gods. The two larger islands were renamed Melita and Gaulos and it has been tentatively suggested that the name Melita was not a Romanized version of the Phoenician Malet, but derived from **mel** (honey) for which the islands were then famous.

With Carthage destroyed in the Third Punic War, and the Greeks overcome, the Mediterranean became a Roman Lake — the Mare Nostrum — the areas of conflict of imperial conquest now being the lands bordering this sea.

The Romans built the city of Melita, itself bearing the same name as that of the island, the city was built over an older, Punic settlement in what is now the Rabat/Mdina area in Malta, and also another town in Gozo under what is now Victoria (Rabat).

Saint Paul

The shipwreck of St. Paul in 60AD is recorded in some detail in the Acts of the Apostles, and a Pauline tradition of long standing supported by archeological excavations carried out at San Pawl Milqghi prove beyond doubt that his arrival in Malta is a historical fact and it is also a fact that during his three-month stay on the Island he sowed the first seeds of the Christian Religion to which Maltese people overwhelmingly belong, but inevitably, a number of legends have grown up over the centuries, some verging on the impossible, but others not without a grain of truth.

The Apostle Paul was, at this time, being conducted to Rome under arrest to be judged before Caesar as was his right as a Roman Citizen. Amongst the other prisoners was the physician St. Luke who recorded the account of that eventual journey.

The nearest habitation to the place of shipwreck was the villa of Publius, the Chief Man of the Island, all those who had been shipwrecked spent three days there and after they had regained their strength they moved on to Melita the chief town of the island. In the city Paul cured Publius' father of a fever after which the Chief Man of the Island was converted to Christianity and later ordained Bishop by St. Paul. St. Publius being the first bishop of Malta.

After three months, by which time, the sea was again reckoned to be safe for navigation, and loaded with gifts from his Maltese friends, Saint Paul sailed away to Rome and to his subsequent martyrdom. When the Roman Emperor Constantine embraced Christianity and made it the official religion of the Empire it may be assumed that Christian worship was better organised and that a number of places of assembly were built in various places in the islands. Tradition has it that one such church was built on the site of the palace of Publius, where St. Paul had cured the father of the Chief Man of the Island. Many times rebuilt, the site is now occupied by the Cathedral Church dedicated to Saint Paul at Mdina.

An Empire in Decline

When the Roman Empire had been divided between the two sons of the Emperor Theodosius, Malta and its islands came under the Empire of the East which had its capital in remote Byzantium (modern day Istanbul). Very little is known of Maltese history regarding the four centuries starting from around the year 400AD. This was the period of the break-up of the old Roman Empire, the time when Vandals and Goths carried all before them in Spain and in North Africa and, indeed, on the Italian mainland, the City of Rome itself was taken.

About the middle of the 6th Century the lands under Byzantine domination were organised into a series of military provinces or **Themes**.

The Arabs

The Arab attacks on the islands started from around the year

836 during which time Malta and its islands were still under Byzantine rule, but the islands were only overcome in the year 870 by Aglabid Arabs originating from what is now Tunisia who used Sicily as a springboard for their invasion, that island having been occupied by them some thirty years previously.

To better protect their new territories the Moslems sectioned off a part of the old Roman town of Melita and defended it with a ditch, calling this citadel **Mdina**, and did the same thing to the capital of the sister island, Gozo; the élite of the small number of Arabs, then on the islands, probably dwelt in these towns but Arab villages were scattered on both islands; such as **Baħrija** in Malta (baħarija: Arabic for oasis) and the village of **Għarb** in Gozo (għarb: Arabic for West — that hamlet being the most westerly of the Maltese Islands).

The name of the two principal islands, Melita and Gaulos, were changed to Malta and Għawdex and two of the smaller islands were named Kemmuna and Filfla, named after the cummin seed and peppercorn respectively. The Arabs introduced the water-wheel, the **sienja**, an animal-driven device for raising water, now practically obsolete, and, much more importantly, the cultivation of the cotton-plant, the mainstay of the Maltese economy for several centuries.

The Middle Ages

The Arabs in Sicily were divided, and taking advantage of the situation, Count Roger the Norman, after a series of compaigns, subdued that island to Norman Rule.

Count Roger had invaded the islands to make sure his southern flank was secure from a possible Arab attack, having reduced the Arabs to a state of vassalage and releasing the foreign Christian slaves, he returned to Sicily without even bothering to garrison his prize.

In Sicily itself the Normans followed the same enlighted policy and although the Christian Faith was regarded as the official religion there, nobody was persecuted because of his race or for his religious beliefs.

In 1127, Roger II the son of Count Roger, led a second invasion of Malta; having overrun the Island he placed it under a more secure Norman domination under the charge of a Norman governor, he also garrisoned with Norman soldiers the three castles then on the islands.

Because the last Norman king died without a male heir, the new masters of the Maltese islands came, in turn, from the ruling houses of Germany, France and Spain: The Swabians (1194); the Angevins (1268); the Aragonese (1283) and finally, the Castillians (1410).

When the Norman Period came to an end, the Fief of Malta was granted to loyal servants of the Sicilian Crown; these Counts, or Marquises of Malta, as these nobles were styled, looked on the fief simply as an investment — a source for the collection of taxes and something that was bartered or sold when no longer viable.

The last feudal lord of Malta, Don Gonsalvo Monroy, had been expelled from the Island following a revolt and at the Court of Sicily the count demanded that the strongest measures be taken against the insurgents. At the same Court the representatives of the Maltese offered to repay the 30,000 florins originally paid by Monroy for the Fief of Malta; they also asked for the Island to be incorporated in the Royal Domains once they had redeemed their homeland. The king, Alphonse V, impressed by their loyalty, called Malta the most **notable** gem in his crown, thus the capital of Malta came to be called Notabile although, then, as now, the Maltese continued to call the town Mdina.

By this time, the Maltese were thoroughly Christianized and the houses of the great Religious Orders were being established in the Island: the Franciscans (1370); the Carmelites (1418); the Augustinians (1450); the Dominicans (1466); and the Minor Observants (1492), while the Benedictine Sisters arrived in 1418.

In 1429 a determined attempt was made by an army of 18,000 Moors from Tunisia under Kaid Ridavan to capture the Maltese islands with the intention of using them as an advance post for further conquests. The Maltese population then numbered between 16,000 to 18,000 with only some 4,000 men under arms. The invaders were beaten back but not before they had captured over 3,000 of the inhabitants as prisoners.

The Knights of the Order of St. John

The visitor arriving by air will probably first notice it in the livery colours of Air Malta, the national airline; he will see it again and again during his stay on the Island: carved on the façade of Baroque palaces, in the form of exquisite filigree brooches, and embossed on many a kitsch, plastic souvenir. It is Eight-pointed, or, as it is better known, the Maltese Cross.

As a military order, the Knights took part in the crusading wars, but when Acre fell in 1291, they were driven off from their last stronghold in the Holy Land.

After a short stay in Cyprus, the Knights, with the assistance of the Genoese, occupied Rhodes. This was to be their home for the next two hundred years.

After wandering for seven years the Knights, and the Rhodian refugees that had attached themselves to them, were offered the Island of Malta for a home by the Holy Roman Emperor, Charles V.

To the relief of the Maltese Nobles, the Knights decided that Mdina, the capital city, was too far inland and they set about establishing themselves in the small village that had grown up behind the old Castel à Mare.

In Birgu the Knights organized themselves along the lines they had evolved during their stay in Rhodes.

The Order could be described as a multi-national force divided into **Langues** according to the nationality of its members, these langues, or **tongues**, were: Auvergne, Provence, France, Aragon, Castile, England, Germany and Italy. Each langue had its own **Auberge**, or headquarters, as well as a specific duty traditionally assigned to it, each langue was also responsible for the defence of a particular post, such as a section of a bastion or tower.

As if to prove the inadequacy of the defences of the islands, in 1547, and again in 1551, the Turks launched two attacks against the islands, the latter being particularly calamitous. Ravaging the Maltese countryside and ignoring the fortified

towns, the Turks then turned their attention to the island of Gozo and carried away the entire population into slavery.

That same year the Turks drove the Knights out of Tripoli. These attacks stung the Knights into feverish activity to improve the islands' defences in anticipation of another, and possibly bigger, attack.

The Great Siege

"Nothing is better known than the siege of Malta" wrote Voltaire two hundred years after the event, and for the Maltese people today the statement still rings true.

The bare bones of the narrative are as follows:

On the 18th May, 1565, the Ottoman Turks and their allies pitted 48,000 of their best troops against the islands with the intention of invading them, and afterwards to make a thrust into Southern Europe by way of Sicily and Italy.

Against them were drawn up some 8,000 men: 540 Knights; 4,000 Maltese; and the rest made up of Spanish and Italian mercenaries.

Landing unopposed, the first objective of the Turks was to secure a safe anchorage for their large invasion fleet, and with that in mind, launched their attack on St. Elmo. After a heroic resistence of thirtyone days the fort succumbed to the massive bombardment and continuous attacks of the Turks. After the fort had been reduced, the Ottomans turned their attention to the two badly fortified towns overlooking the harbour. Subjected to a ceaseless bombardment, and repulsing attack after attack; behind the crumbling walls, the Christian forces, against all odds, kept the enemy at bay until a small relief force of some 8,000 troops arrived from Sicily (a smaller relief force of 600 men had previously landed at about the time that St. Elmo had fallen).

The Foundation of Valletta

The idea of fortifying the rocky and steep-sided Mount Sciberras had occured to the Knights on their arrival in 1530, but because time was not on their side, they limited themselves to building a fort at its very tip, instead.

If other Grand Masters studied the possibilities of such a project, La Valette was obsessed with the idea; as soon as he had been elected to the Grand Mastership in 1557 he invited foreign military engineers, famous in their time, to prepare the plans, but the Great Siege put a stop to all that.

No sooner was the siege lifted that the plans for the fortress city were again revived, but as a first step the ill-fated Fort St.

Elmo was at once rebuilt.

Pope Pius IV sent his military engineer, Francesco Laparelli, and the planning of the new town started in earnest.

When Laparelli departed from the Island he left his Maltese assistant, Gerolamo Cassar, to continue the work he had started. La Valette died in 1568 and was buried in the Church of Our Lady of Victories, the first building to be erected. Other Grand Masters continued to embellish the new city and, in time, all the important buildings of the Order were enclosed within its walls: the Auberges of the Langues of the Order; the Grand Master's Palace with its Armoury; the Co-Cathedral and other churches; the Hospital; the Courts of Justice and the palatial houses of individual Knights, rich Maltese citizens, and ecclesiastics.

The Fall of the Order

When the Order made Malta its home, for the first time the masters of the Maltese lived on the Island itself, and wealth poured **into** the Island, rather than the other way round.

The finances of the Order were now in a precarious position. Unemployment was rife and poverty was widespread.

Towards the end of the 18th Century matters for the Order were going from bad to worse: in France, where most of her overseas property lay, the possessions of the Order were taken over by the Republican Government and French refugees, fleeing to Malta from the Revolution, were an added drain on the treasury of the Order.

At the time the last Grand Master of Malta, Ferdinand von Hompesch, was being elected, Napoleon was making his plans to take over the Island.

The French

Napoleon's capture of Malta in June 1798 cannot be counted as one of his military triumphs.

The Grand Master capitulated without offering any resistence and Napoleon made his grand entry into Valletta and within a week Von Hompesch, accompanied by a few knights, left the Island unwept, unhonoured, and unsung.

The Maltese felt that they had been led down by the Order, but before they could attempt any resistence they were talked into submission by the Bishop. Maltese that had served in the Order's army and navy were recruited into the French Republican forces, and other regiments were raised for garrison duties on the Island itself.

After stripping the palaces, Auberges and other buildings of everything of value, Napoleon, conveniently forgetting his promises, next turned his attention to the churches; only such articles that were indispensable for the "exercise of the cult" were left while all other valuables were removed and priceless works of art in gold and silver melted down into lingots.

Nominally the Order had held the Island of Malta in fief from the King of Sicily (since 1735 this island had been amalgamated with the State of Naples and was then known as the Kingdom of the Two Sicilies), and it was to the King of the Two Sicilies that the Maltese now turned for aid and protection. At the same time deputies were despatched to seek aid from the allies of the King, the British.

A small number of British troops were landed and the French in Gozo surrendered in October 1798, the Sicilian flag being hoisted on the ramparts.

As the siege wore on, the French penned in the fortifications were prevented from receiving aid because of the British blockade, while the Maltese, by this time, aided by Italian and British troops, did not have the means of assaulting the formidable bastions.

The French, having arrived at the end of their tether, were ready to capitulate but the troops of Napoleon proudly refused to submit to the Maltese rebels.

The British, on the other hand, anxious to deploy their troops and warships in other theatres of war, were eager to speed up the surrender of the French in Malta.

The National Congress was dissolved and the Maltese Battalions disbanded; a Maltese regiment formed by the British, under British officers was, however, retained.

The British

Once the French were expelled from the Island, the British were not so much interested in keeping Malta, as keeping the French out, in fact, at the Treaty of Amiens (1802), that brought hostilities between Britain and Frrance to an end, it was decided that Malta was to be returned to a reformed Order of St. John under the protection of the Kingdom of the Two Sicilies and that her neutrality was to be guaranteed by all the Great Powers.

With the British in command of the sea, all mercantile shipping was obliged to call at the Valletta Harbour for clearance by the British Navy, and before long, the Maltese Islands became the most important centre of trade in the Mediterranean.

Under the Treaty of Paris (1814) the Island was confirmed as a British Possession.

As steam replaced sail, Malta became an important coaling station, all the more so after the opening of the Suez Canal in 1869. The dockyards were expanded and provided work for a sizeable section of the population. Agriculture was encouraged to make the Island Fortress as self-sufficient as possible and the growing of potatoes, now a major agricultural export, was introduced. The ever present problem of the water supply also received urgent attention.

Prosperity brought about a rapid rise in the population and emigration was activelv encouraged to ease the burden on the Italian political refugees of the **Risorgimento** sought refuge in Malta and the example of these Italian patriots had the effect of further fanning the flames of Maltese Nationalism.

At the insistence of the Maltese a Council of Government was set up in 1835.

The military worth of Malta and its islands was to be demonstrated during the Crimean War (1854-56) when the Island Fortress became a rear base for the departure of troops and a receiving station for casualties.

Imperial policy dictated that Britain take Malta under its wing and anglicize, as far as possible, the local population. Before long, the Language Question, as it came to be called, lost its shibboleth value and the fight resolved itself on which of the two languages, English or Italian, were to be taught in Government schools. The Maltese tongue, the language of the people, was to receive a welcome boost from the pro-British faction which promoted the vernacular in favour of Italian as a second language.

In the meantime the question of proper representation was inching slowly towards self-determination.

The First World War placed Malta on a war footing and, as happened in the Crimean War sixty years earlier, Malta was to provide harbour and dockyard facilities to the Allied Navies and her contribution in the cause of sick and wounded soldiers hospitalized on the Island earned Malta the title "Nurse of the Mediterranean".

A National Assembly was set up to make proposals for a new constitution. During one of the public meetings of this Assembly, held on the 7th June 1919, the crowd grew hostile and the troops were called out to restore order. When the troops opened fire on the rioters, three of them were killed while another died of his wounds later. With the new Constitution, that of 1921, Malta was, at last, to be granted Self-Government with responsibility for all internal affairs. The British Government retained control on Defence; Foreign Affairs; and Immigration.

The Path to Independence

For the Maltese People the path to independence was neither smooth nor straight.

By the time Malta was granted Self-Government in 1921 the political factions could be classified into three main groups: the pro-British group that broadly opted for the advancement of the English language and culture, as well as the dissemination of the Maltese language. The pro-Italian group stood for the use of Italian and English but also for the propagation of Italian culture.

A newcomer to the political scene was the Labour Party, then in its infancy,its programme being compulsory education, the promotion of the English and Maltese languages and, as is to be expected, the improvement of working and social conditions.

In the troubles that followed elections were suspended and the Constitution was withdrawn in 1930.

In the following election the pro-Italian party with the support of the Church won at the polls with a great majority. In the political storm that followed the Constitution was again suspended and, one year later, Malta reverted back to colonial rule. The British Government, now in sole control of the Island and unfettered by local political opinion, made Maltese and English the two official languages of the Island, which, in fact, they still are, while the use of Italian was eliminated from administrative circles.

By the time the next constitution was granted World War II had started. When Italy allied herself to Germany Malta was thrown into the front line. The first attack, by Italian bombers, took place on the 11th June 1940. The exodus from the towns into the countryside started soon afterwards.

Using ancient catacombs and a disused railway tunnel as shelters against air-raids, other tunnels were excavated in the living rock for the same purpose. War in the Mediterranean theatre was predictable, yet when it did come the Island was poorly equipped to defend itself: the only fighter planes were four antiquated Gloster Gladiators. These planes were augmented with a few Hurricanes some weeks later. Against these, the Italian **Regia Aeronautica** could count on two hundred aircraft stationed in Sicily, a mere hundred kilometres from Malta.

As a result many buildings, especially those in the harbour area and near the airfields were flattened or badly damaged.

In June 1941 Hitler attacked Russia and the **Luftwaffe** in Sicily diverted most of its planes to that front. The air-raids on Malta eased, but did not cease entirely; at the same time, having received reinforcements, Malta took to the offensive and submarines and aircraft based on the Island attacked Axis shipping as well as ground targets in Sardinia, Sicily and even Tripoli; furthermore, by intercepting supplies from Sicily to North Africa, Rommel was deprived of many essential supplies. On 26th July 1941 the only seaborne attack, that directed against the Grand Harbour by Italian E-boats, was brave and dashing, but unsucessful. It was radar that had alerted the Maltese gunners and foiled the E-boat attack.

When the **Luftwaffe** was again in Sicily in full complement the bombing commenced once more and Malta was, once again, thrown on the defensive. Munition, fuel and other stores were running low and food was in short supply.

Throughout this ordeal, despite continuous air-raids, lack of practically all necessities, and an acute food shortage, the Maltese soldiered on. A third of the anti-craft crews were Maltese and they soon made a name for themselves for their bravery and efficiency.

On the 15th of April 1942 King George VI awarded the George Cross Medal to "… the brave people of the Island Fortress of Malta".

If the morale of Malta's defenders was high, the material resources of the Island were low; with supply ships being intercepted and destroyed by Axis aircraft and submarines the situation was desperate, by July 1942 the supply of vital provisions was calculated to last two weeks. Although badly mauled, the "Santa Maria Convoy" limped into the Grand Harbour on the 15th August of that year and the situation was saved.

With replenished stores and the arrival of some hundred Spitfires, the tables, at last, were being turned.

Although Malta was still under attack, by June 1943, it was considered sufficiently safe for King George to visit the Island to a huge welcome by the Maltese people whom he had so singularly honoured.

A month later, using Malta as an advance base, the Allies invaded Sicily and the war moved away from the Island.

True to their promise made during the War, the British restored Self-Government.

Fresh elections were held and the pro-Italian exiles were repatriated. With most of the inhabitants being homeless, reconstruction was the first priority of the newly elected Labour Government but social conditions were also improved.

In the dockyard area, especially, the trade union movement grew in strength as workers everywhere were becoming conscious of their rights.

Three years later, following a split in the Labour Party, the Nationalist Party headed a Coalition Government, this party now strove to obtain a Dominion Status for the Island. The

Nationalists were formerly the pro-Italian party but, since the post-war years, the image of this party was to change gradually and in the end they were even accused of being pro-British! Originally being the party of the intelligentsia, the party now attracted numerous workers within its ranks.

On the return of the Labour Party to office, a request for integration was made to the British Government with Maltese representation at Westminster. When the British cooled to the idea after evincing an initial interest the Labour Party went to the other extreme and insisted on Independence, and the Church was accused of having undermined the Integration plan by insisting that its ancient privileges be safeguarded; the acrimonies that followed were to cost the Labour Party many votes.

The Constitutional Party, the original pro-British party, died a natural death, its mission having been accomplished.

In the wake of fresh elections and confirmed by a referendum, Malta achieved Independence within the Commonwealth on 21st September 1964 with the Queen of England as the nominal Queen of Malta.

Under the next Labour Government, Malta was declared a Republic with Sir Anthony Mamo as its first President.

On the 31st March 1979, at the termination of the Military Base Agreement, the last British serviceman left the Island and Malta entered into its self-imposed state of neutrality.

The tourism was promoted and foreign investors were encouraged to set up factories in Malta.

"In the 1987 elections, the Nationalists were returned to power and although adhereing to the concept of neutrality, they made it their declared policy of applying for membership in the EU and with that in view, Government legislation was enacted and amended to conform with European standards in anticipation of forming part of the Community.

In October 1996 the Labour Party, under the leadership of Dr Alfred Sant, was elected to Government with a clear policy of maintaining and strengthening close co-operation with the EU but stopping short of membership".

Valletta

When Grand Master Jean Parisot de la Valette laid the foundation stone of **Humilissima Civitas Vallettae** the last thing that he had in mind was a city of fine palaces, Valletta was intended as a fortress to protect the two harbours on either side of the rocky peninsula on which it was to be built.

The first buildings to be erected were the Auberges, these were the headquarters of the different ethnic groups into which the Knights were divided.

The National Library, the **Biblioteca**, was the last building to have been built by the Order having been finished in 1796. It houses a rich collection of books as well as medieval manuscripts and the archives of the Order. As a memento one can buy a photocopy of the deed of Emperor Charles V in which he granted Malta and its islands in fief to the Order in 1530.

Even if the Opera House has yet to rise from the ashes of the Blitz (some are of the opinion that a multi-storey car park should be built there instead), music lovers and balletomanes can still go to Manoel Theatre. This gem of a building was built in 1732 and has recently been restored to its former glory for, as its builder Grand Master Anton Manoel de Vilhena would have said it, "... the honest recreation of the people". For art lovers there are the Museum of Fine Arts and the Cathedral Museum.

Valletta boasts of three Parish Churches and a host of others, but pride of place must go to St. John's Co-Cathedral.

The plain exterior of this edifice grossly belies its sumptuous interior: no space is left unadorned, the walls are carved and gilt and the painted vaulted ceiling is the masterpiece of Mattia Preti while fourhundred slabs of inlaid marble pave the church, these slabs are emblazoned with the armorial bearings of the more important members of the Order.

In years gone by, people, young people especially, used to troop into Valletta every evening; they filled the many cinemas there, crowded the coffee shops or just strolled up and down the main streets to admire and be admired, followed by a last-minute rush to catch the last bus to the village.

The Grand Masters' Palace

Valletta is a city of palaces but for the Maltese, the Grand Masters' Palace is known simply as il-Palazz, **the** Palace.

In its finished form the Palace is built on two floors and occupies an entire block. The two main portals, Baroque and imposing, stand in direct contrast to the unadorned treatment of the rest of the façade; three other side entrances give on to as many streets.

Three of the doorways lead to a spacious courtyard while another portal and a gate lead to a smaller courtyard which is on a slightly higher level. The larger of the two courtyards is known as Neptune's Courtyard from a bronze statue of that god. The smaller courtyard — Prince Alfred's Courtyard is named after one of Queen Victoria's sons to commemorate his visit to Malta in 1858, but this courtyard is better known as that of Pinto's Clock. This clock has four dials showing, besides the time: the day, the month and the phases of the moon. The hours are struck by bronze effigies of Moorish slaves wielding sledge-hammers. It is said to be the work of the Maltese clockmaker Gaetano Vella and built in 1745.

As in Renaissance palaces in Italy, the important storey was the **Piano Nobile**, the first floor; the ground floor be-

Entrance to the Grand Masters Palace

ing used as stables, service quarters and stores.

The Main Staircase leading up to the **Piano Nobile** was built by Grand Master Hughes de Loubenx Verdala as advertised by the wolf in his coat of arms. The top of the staircase gives on to a lobby formed by the angle where two fo the palace corridors meet.

The right-hand passage leads to what used to be the Palace Armoury but that part of the building is now the seat of the House of Representatives (the Parliamentary Assembly is composed of only one chamber, there is no Upper House).

The lunettes over the windows in this passage are the work of Nicolò Nasoni da Siena and have been painted in the first quarter of the 18th Century. Their opposite numbers have been painted by the Maltese artist Giovanni Bonello some hundred and sixty years later; the whole set, however, is complementary and shows Maltese and Gozitan landscapes as they appeared at those times.

A notable hall in the Armoury Corridor is the Council, or Tapestry, Chamber, which was the place where the members of the Order seat in Council. This chamber was also the seat of the Malta Parliament from 1921 until 1974, before the House moved to its present situation.

On being elected to that high office, a Grand Master was

The Neptune courtyard.

expected to make a gift to the Order — the **Gioja**.

Part of the **Gioja** of Grand Master Ramon Perellos y Rocaful is the priceless set of Gobelins Tapestries that give the name to this chamber. Perellos was elected in 1697 but it was only in 1710 that these tapestries were completed and hung in the place for which they had been created. **Les Tentures des Indes** (the Indian Tapestries) is a vague title for a magnificent rendering of fauna and flora from three continents, the Noble Savage being also very much in evidence.

To the left-hand of the lobby at the top of the Main Staircase is another corridor, known as the Entrance Corridor, this too, like the Armoury Corridor is decorated by paintings of Nicolò Nasini, but this time the subject chosen for the decoration of the lunettes are scenes of naval battles between the Order's galleys and those of the Ottoman Turks, apparently a subject dear to the hearts of these seafaring Knights.

The first door to the right of the lobby leads into the State Dining Room, here the British connection is well represented by several Royal portraits. The next door down the Entrance Corridor leads to the Hall of the Supreme Council, also known as the Throne Room. Like all the other ceilings of the **Piano Nobile**, the wooden ceiling of this hall is elaborately coffered and painted, but the item of greater interest in this hall is a frieze of twelve frescoes by Matteo Perez d'Aleccio who worked in Malta between 1576 and 1581.

Against the far end of the wall is the throne, occupied in turn, by the Grand Masters and the British Governors. Above the throne are now the arms of the Republic of Malta.

Across the hall and opposite the throne a carved minstrels' gallery is let into the wall; this carved and painted gallery is said to have been part of the Order's flagship, the Great Carrack of Rhodes, which was one of the vessels that carried the Knights to Malta.

A door from the Throne Room leads to the Ambassadors' Room, also known as the Red Room from the colour of its damask hanging.

In one of the panels, Knights of the Order are shown holding shields bearing the white eight-pointed (or Maltese) cross on a **red** background; this could be poetic licence on the part of the painter because the battle standard of the

Order was a plain white cross on a red background, something like the Danish Flag. A door from the Ambassadors' Room leads to the **Paggeria**, the Pages' waiting room, also known as the Yellow Room from the gold damask covering of its walls.

A door from the Pages' Waiting Room leads into a corridor which is at a right angle to the Entrance Corridor. This corridor is known as the Prince of Wales Corridor in commemoration of a visit by King Edward VII, then Prince of Wales, in 1862.

The rooms giving on to this passage were formerly the private apartment of the Grand Master, afterwards they were used as the offices of the British Governors. These rooms are now the offices of the President of the Republic.

The private chapel of the Grand Master was turned into an office for the use of the Governor's Secretary and the minstrels' gallery that was in it, removed to the Throne Room where it still is. The paintings in this chapel are probably the earliest found in the palace and show episodes from the life of St. John the Baptist, the patron saint of the Order that bears its name.

The armours of the Knights of Malta

The collection, as presently displayed, is small but interesting; in the old Armoury, and even more so in engravings of the Armoury as it was at one time, one is impressed by the great number of exhibits, but on the other hand, many of the specimen were repetitous, to the serious student a specimen collection is more interesting.

At the time of the arrival of the Order in Malta, in 1530, the use of firearms was well on the way of revolutionizing warfare — the Great Siege was fought largely with artillery and arquebus but armour still had its uses — a century later breastplates and shields were still being tested against firearms — in the Armoury there are several examples with dents in them to prove that they were proof against ball, in other words "bulletproof".

The main entrance to the upper floor with the coat-of-arms of the Malta Republic in the foreground.

The Throne
Room and the
Tapestry
Chamber with
the Gobelins
Tapestries
named "Les
Tentures des
Indes".

C E HOSPITALARI RESTAVRANO VNA PARTE DELLE
MVRRA DI GERVSALEM L'ANNO M.CCXXVIII.

On the top, in the Yellow Room a pannel by Matteo Perez d'Aleccio showing the Hospitallers repairing the Walls of Jerusalem. Bottom, in the Ambassadors' Room a painting shows the Knights leaving from Rhodes.

IL GRĀ M. FR. FILIPPO DI VILLERS LISLEADAMO CON LI SVOI
HOSPITALARY SI PARTE DA RODI L'ANNO 1522.

St. John's Co-Cathedral

In 1573 Grand Master Jean de la Cassière authorized the construction of a conventual church of the Order of St. John. It was completed in 1578 by the Maltese architect Girolamo Cassar. Alessandro Algardi's bas relief of the Saviour surmounting the façade was relocated here in 1850's from its original place in a chapel close to the entrance of the Grand Harbour. The spires on the bell towers were destroyed during the Second World War.

The rectangular Baroque interior was embellished by successive Grandmasters and further enriched by the "Gioja" or present, which every Knight was bound by statute to give on admission to the Order.

Between 1662-67, Mattia Preti "Il Calabrese" painted the life of St. John the Baptist, patron saint of the Order, directly on to the primed stone of the ceiling. The Cottoner brothers paid for this work.

In the ornate Oratory is a 3 by 5 metre painting by Caravaggio depicting the beheading of St. John. This painting is regarded as the master piece of Caravaggio and is the only one of his paintings which bears his signature.

Above: dedicatory monument to Grand Master Emmanuel Pinto in the St. James Chapel. Below is the splendid organ also standing in the Oratory of the Beheading.

The "Beheading of St. John", one of the last works of Caravaggio done in 1608, is on display inside the Oratory.

Auberge de Provence

The Auberge de Provence was built between 1571-75 to a design of the Maltese architect Girolamo Cassar. The façade was re-designed during the first half of the 18th Century. The Auberge was the residence of the Langue de Provence, its Head, the "Grand Commandeur" being the Treasurer of the Order.

From 1824 to 1954 the building housed the British officers' Union Club, and is now the National Museum of Archeology. It contains a rich collection of prehistoric artefacts such as pottery, statuettes, stone implements, personal and other ornaments recovered from Malta's prehistoric and megalithic temple sites. Several table models of these temples are on permanent exhibition. Tomb furniture from the Punic and Roman periods are also displayed.

Ceramic Pottery of the early Phoenician-Punic Period (7th Century B.C.).

On the top is a limestone statuette from the megalithic temples of Hagar Qim; below the Venus of Malta.

Photo on the top: Etruscan cinenary urn (3rd — 2nd century B.C.).
Below: Terracotta masks (6th — 5th century B.C.).
Next page, on the top: a limestone Punic funenary stele from Carthage (3rd century B.C.).
Below: Schematic sculpture removed from a Punic rock-cut tomb at Qallilija.

National Museum of Fine Arts

South Street is one of the most elegant streets in the city. It was originally known as Strada del Palazzo after the Magisterial Palace which was to be built here. This street was also known as Strada d'Albergo di Francia after the Auberge de France, destroyed during the last war, situated in it.

The National Museum of Fine Arts is one of the palaces gracing this street. This was among the first buildings erected in Valletta but it was rebuilt in its present form between 1761 and 1765. During the French occupation it was offered to the Bishop of Malta to be used as a seminary. On the capitulation of the French garrison, "Casa Miari" as the palace then became known, was occupied by the Commander of the Anglo-Maltese troops, Captain Alexander Ball.

In 1808, Louis Charles Viscount de Beaujolais, and his brother Louis Philippe, Duke of Orléans arrived in Malta on board the French warship "Voltaire". They were

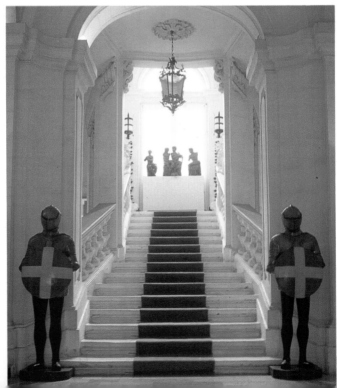

lodged in this palace and it was here that the Viscount de Beaujolais died.

The premises were leased to the British naval authorities in 1821 and the palace remained the official residence of the Commander-in-Chief of the British Mediterranean Fleet. Amongst the famous admirals who occupied these premises we find Suffren de Saint Tropez, Cordington of Navarino, Fisher of Kilverstone, Keyes of Zeebrugge, Cunninghan of Hyndhope and Mountbatten of Burma.

In 1961 it was handed to the Maltese Gouvernment and in 1974 it was restored to its former glory and converted into a Museum of Fine Arts. It houses paintings, sculpture, furniture and objects connected with the Order of St. John. Permanently displayed in this Museum are works by Reni, Valentini, Stormer, Preti, Tiepolo, Favray and Perugino. A section is specially reserved for works by Maltese artists. Temporary exhibitions and lectures are also held here.

Madonna and Child, from the Florentine School of the 16th Century.
On the next page: Christ holding the Cross by Guido Reni (1575-1642).

Auberge of Castille

The Auberge of Castille, Leon and Portugal, is the largest and perhaps finest of all the Auberges. Its head was the Grand Chancellor of the Order of St. John.

It was first built in 1574 by Girolamo Cassar on a site originally earmarked for the Magisterial Palace. Extensive reconstructions were undertaken in 1744 during Grand Master Pinto de Fonseca's term of office. Domenico Cachia, the architect responsible for these modifications was influenced by the Prefettura at Lecce and produced a very imposing façade.

Among the various monuments housed in the Upper Barracca gardens, it is interesting to observe the bronze work "Les Gavroches" of the Maltese sculptor Antonio Sciortino (bottom on the next page).

The Three Cities

Collectively known as the Three Cities, individually, the towns by the harbour are known by several names; however, Birgu, Bormla and Senglea are the names by which they are most commonly known.

In the beginning there was Birgu, then a small fishing village sheltering behind a castle of unknown antiquity that stood at the very tip of the peninsula. The castle, as the Castrum Maris, or Castell 'a Mare, is mentioned in several medieval documents. Apparently the Castellan had a measure of autonomy and was independent of the **Università**, the municipal council with its seat at Mdina, and it also appears that the people whose houses were outside the wall of this castle considered themselves as being under the jurisdiction of the Castellan and beyond that of the **Università** which led to much bad blood between the two bodies.

On their arrival in 1530 the Knights decided to settle in Birgu as Mdina was too far inland, and immediately set

Below: the ancient Hospital of Bighi

about protecting that hamlet with bastions. Castell 'a Mare was strengthened and separated from Birgu by a ditch. Not long afterwards, the adjacent peninsula, then uninhabited and known as l'Isla was likewise protected bu bastions and by the time Claude de la Sengle was Grand Master it was sufficiently inhabited to merit the name of "Città Senglea" named, of course, after the Grand Master.

During the Great Siege of 1565 the inhabitants of Birgu and Senglea showed such outstanding courage that the two towns received the honorific titles of Città Vittoriosa (the Victorious City), and Città Invitta (the Unconquered City) respectively.

The conurbation that linked Birgu and Senglea was named "Bormla" and as successive Grand Masters enclosed all three cities with imposing lines of bastions, Bormla received the title of Città Cospicua (the Noteworthy). As Valletta was being built, the Knights transferred their seat of government from Birgu to that town but the three cities were still very much the centre of the naval ac-

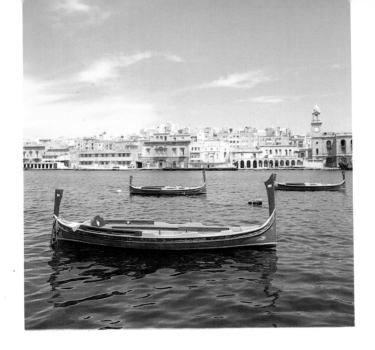

tivities of the Order; here were the shipyards and the arsenals, and here lived the Maltese seamen and ship chandlers.

Piracy was a profession of long standing, but with the arrival of the Order, Maltese corsairs achieved respectability by operating under licence from the Grand Master; and by being taxed on their booty!

Merchants of several nationalities lived in the Three Cities and traded in slaves and other merchandise acquired by the corsairs and galleys of the Order. The cosmopolitan character of the Three Cities is still discernible: there are more "foreign" Maltese surnames in this part of the Island than in any other.

Under the British, the Three Cities were a hive of activity as the Grand Harbour became the home base of the British Mediterranean Fleet, and at the same time several rich Maltese shipowning families settled in Birgu and Senglea. The docks were enlarged and increased in number and the Castell 'a Mare, which the Knights had renamed Sant Antelo, now became a shore establishment of the Navy under the name of H.M.S. St. Angelo.

Being in close proximity to military installations, the Three Cities suffered terribly as a result of enemy bombing, Senglea in particular. The inhabitants were evacuated to the relative safety of the countryside but many a historic building was irreparably destroyed.

With the granting of Indipendence and the subsequent closing down of the military base (a tableau in bronze recreates the farewell ceremony), oil tankers and freighters have replaced destroyers and cruisers in the dockyards.

Birgu, despite the Blitz, still has a lot to offer the visitor, such as a number of 16th Century houses in which the Knights made their abode on their arrival; the Inquisitor's Palace which incorporates a Folk Museum; and the magnificent Church of St. Lawrence.

For the more active, a walk around the bastions of Senglea with a camera can be rewarding.

Above the Fort St. Angelo at Vittoriosa and below the "Couvre Porte" gate which leads into Vittoriosa.

Above: a sight of Senglea

Characteristic foreshortening

Tarxien Temples

In no other site in Malta is the evolution of prehistoric temple building better exemplified than it is at the megalithic temples of Tarxien. The earliest temple, now unfortunately in a vestigial state, goes back to around 2,800BC while the more recent of the four temples burst out in a blaze of splendour some seven hundred years later. The spiral, as a decorative motif, is found in many places in Europe from the North Atlantic seaboard to the Aegean; the ones at Tarxien, however, might have been invented, or at least developed, independently. Inside these temples has been found what, for that age, was the most colossal stone sculpture then in existence; originally 2.50 metres in height, the statue, presumably representing a Mother Goddess, has been broken in half and the top part is missing. There is a lot of conjecture about the significance of the Fat Lady statues found in most of the Maltese temples, it is possible that they are examples of female fertility deities prevalent throughout the lands bordering the Mediterranean. Around 1,800BC the temples, having been abandoned for about two hundred years, were reused by Bronze Age folk as crematoria and as repositories of the ashes of their dead.

Marsaxlokk

Marsaxlokk, the harbour to the south-east, is now a small but picturesque harbour where the brightly coloured fishing boats ride at anchor and where the wives of the fishermen knot nylon string bags for the tourists.

But Marsaxlokk is also a microcosm of the historical past of the Island. A short distance from this village is the archeological site of **tas-Silġ**, still in the process of being excavated; at this place are the remains of Late Neolithic megalithic buildings much disturbed by superimposed Punic and Byzantine structures; here too are the only remains of a mosque to be found on the Island. Norman coins have also found at **tas-Silġ**.

To oppose the landing of corsairs in that harbour a fort was erected at its entrance by the Order, that of San Lucian; used as a munition depot during World War II, it now houses the Marine Research Centre. Marsaxlokk Bay, of which the fishing harbour of Marsaxlokk forms part, is now being converted into a port for container ships.

The characteristic Maltese boats anchored in the port of Marsaxlokk. On the following page: the return of the fishermen's boats after a good catch.

Għar Dalam

At the time the Maltese islands were an extension of the Italian mainland, animals like the elephant, hippos, deer and foxes roamed the land. With the rising of the sea-level, or the sinking of the land, or both, the islands were separated from the land mass and these animals were marooned. This took place in the Quaternary Era, some 10,000 years ago, and not during the Pliocene, eleven million to one million years ago, as was once thought to have been the case.

In time these stranded animals gradually evolved into an island sub-race resulting in a degeneration in some of the species.

Fossil bones of animals have been discovered in caves and fissures in various parts of the island, but the largest concentration to be discovered so far is that at Għar Dalam.

In 1917 two human molars were found in this cave and believed, at the time of their discovery, to be those of Neanderthal Man. However, these molars have now been assigned to a much later period and it can be assumed that when the animals died, and their bones carried into Ghar Dalam by the action of flowing water, Man had not yet arrived in Malta. Stone Age Man did use Għar Dalam as his abode around 4,000BC but, by this time these animals had become extinct in the Maltese Islands.

Wied iż - Żurrieq
and the Blue Grotto

The western coast of Malta is steep and precipitous but in places gaps in the cliffs slope down to sea-level. One such gap is Wied iż-Żurrieq. Looking like a miniature fjord, this narrow arm of the sea is an anchorage for boats in calm weather; at the first sign of a storm the boats are winched up a steep slipway and landed.

The boats at Wied iż-Żurrieq were, and still are, used for fishing; now, however, the fishermen are finding out that it is more lucrative to take visitors to the near-by Blue Grotto.

The presence of this deep sea-cave in which the sea bottom is of an unbelievably intense blue has long been known to the fisher folk, in fact, during World War II, when an air-raid alarm was sounded the people here took to their boats and rowed into the cave for safety.

The fishermen from the village of Wied Iż-Żurrieq organize boat trips to admire the fascinating Blue Grotto.

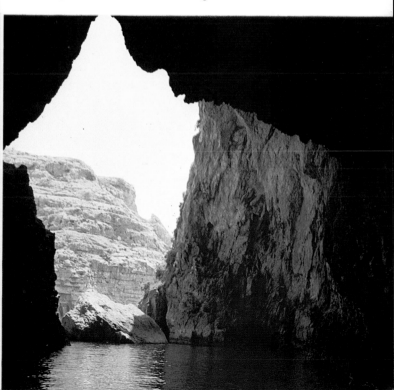

Hagar Qim

This Copper Age temple was originally built about 2,700 BC but during the same period it underwent several modifications. For some unknown reason the axis of the first temple was altered and the temple itself was several times extended.

The kind of stone used in the building of this temple (Globigerina Limestone) is rather solf and relatively simple to work; possibly for this reason there are several "porthole" openings in Ħaġar Qim. A monolith on the outside of the temple wall has been tentatively interpreted as evidence of phallic worship.

A pillar "altar" with an unusual palm frond decorative carving has been found in this temple, but not in any other; it is possible that this pillar was not originally part of the temple furniture and it has been placed there at a later date.

Mnajdra

Perhaps having learned that Globigerina Limestone does not resist weathers the builders of Mnajdra constructed this temple out of the harder Coralline Limestone which, however, was difficult to work, while the interior walls were faced with a softer kind of limestone.

The best preserved of the three Mnajdra temples is interesting for the secret chambers that are hidden inside the thickness of its walls; these chambers communicate with the temple proper by holes bored through the wall; it is surmised that statues of gods, or goddesses, could have been placed in front of these holes and the "priest" hiding in the oracle chamber was the voice of the deity as this "spoke" to the faithful. A healing cult could have been practiced in this temple because a number of baked-clay models of parts of the human body, showing symptoms of disease, have been found here.

Mdina

The citadel they named Mdina (the Town) and the rest of the old settlement they named Rabat (the Suburb), the names by which they are still known.

During the Medieval period Mdina was the seat of the Municipal government and administrative center as well as a mustering station for the militia at the approach of the enemy, while, at the same time, the people from the surrounding countryside took refuge inside its walls.

At this time too, a number of Religious Orders built their monasteries outside the walls of Mdina and established themselves at Rabat and its surroundings. Grim and fortress-like when they were first built, these monasteries are now surrounded by modern buildings and some of them have been modernized beyond recognition.

With the coming of the Order (1530), the Knights found out they would be better served if they established themselves by the harbour where their galleys lay at anchor, and by so doing, they left Mdina and its inhabitants undisturbed. When Valletta was built and eventually became the capital of the Maltese Islands in 1571 Mdina was relegated to that of Città Vecchia (the Old City). Some of the inhabitants of Mdina did migrate to the new city but among those who stayed on were the aristocratic families of Malta who still occupied their ancestral homes there; this had the fortunate effect of preserving a number of old 14th and 15th Century houses and places. The old Maltese aristocratic families owne vast rural property and from time immemorial the farmers came to Mdina to pay their yearly dues to these nobles on the traditional date of the Mnarja (an ancient harvest festival, Christianized into the feast of Saints Peter and Paul).

This feast was, and still is, celebrated under the trees of Malta's nearest thing to a forest, the Buskett. In this place the Grand Masters built a hunting lodge and summer retreat in 1586 known as Verdala Castle. Horse and donkey races are still part of the Mnarja celebrations.

Because Roman Law forbade burials inside the city, the catacombs were located outside the walls of Melita and here too, according to tradition, is the cave in which St. Paul was kept prisoner for three months.

The Main Gate to the City was erected in 1724 by Grand Master de Vilhena, replacing an earlier drawbridge gate the outline of which, now walled up, is still visible some metres away to the right of the present gate. It is reached through a narrow stone bridge, over a moat dug out by the Arabs, and decorated with stone trophies of arms supported by lions — the lion forms part of Grand Master Vilhena's escutcheon.

On the outside are a Latin inscription giving the date and some details on the new gate's erection, a trophy beautiful carved in stone and decorated with martial and triumphal symbols and with the Grand Master's arms on white marble, and on top the coat-of-arms of the city of Mdina and again that of Vilhena.

On the inside the Latin inscription commemorates Antonio Inguanez who in 1428 quelled a rebellion as well as his coat-of-arms.

Bas-relief carvings of stone recall the patron saints of the city: St Paul, St Publius and St Agatha.

A Roman headless marble statue, now in the Museum of Roman Antiquites, was once encased in the wall of the main entrance.

Cathedral Church

According to tradition Malta's earliest Cathedral was dedicated to the Blessed Virgin, Mother of God, dilapidated in the Muslim period and reconstructed and rededicated to St Paul after the Norman conquest.

This old church was modified and enlarged several times. In 1419 a horizontal rectangular wing was added to the edifice; in 1626 Bishop Baldassare Cagliares added a recess at the back and in 1679 Bishop Molina laid the first stone of the choir which was inaugurated on 28 June 1682. The terrible earthquake of 11 January 1693 destroyed the old Cathedral almost completely except for the sacristy and the newly constructed choir. The latter had already been decorated with a fine altarpiece, a canvas representing St Paul's Conversion and a fresco depicting St Paul's Shipwreck as well as five other canvases, all painted by Mattia Preti (1613-1699). These fortunately survived the earthquake.

The reconstruction of a larger Cathedral in the new baroque style was immediately taken in hand and entrusted to the Maltese architect Lorenzo Gafa' who eleven years before had constructed the apsed choir. There was no need for a new plan: Gafa' had previously submitted plan and wooden model for a church in the new baroque style and the Cathedral Chapter had examined and approved them on 18 may 1692, that is eight months before the earthquake had taken place. The new Cathedral was completed and consecrated in October 1702 by Bishop Cocco Palmieri (1684-1713) whose coat-of-arms along with those of the reigning Grand Master Fra Ramon Perellos (1697-1720) and of the City of Mdina were placed on the facade over the main entrance.

Characteristic foreshortening

Cathedral Museum

The Cathedral Museum in Archbishop Square is an imposing baroque palace housing rich collections of art and archaeology as well as important archives. The building, completed in 1744, was constructed as a Diocesan Seminary and served its purpose up to the first decade of the present century; it was then utilized by various ecclesiastical and educational institutions until on 5 january 1969 it was inaugurated by Sir Maurice Dorman, Governor-General of Malta, as the Cathedral's Museum. The main bulk of the art collections is a legacy by Count Saverio Marchese (1757-1833).

A newly opened large room on the right of the entrance serves for the temporary display of new acquisitions but the room is also offered to local artists for exhibiting their latest works and holding one-man exhibitions.

Rabat

Both Rabat and Mdina are perched on a ridge dominating the whole expanse of the island and of the sea beyond. Both have been a centre of habitation for thousands of years.

Rabat incorporates a good part of the old Roman city which was reduced to its present outline by the Arabs. This explains how the sumptuous townhouse with its fine polychrome mosaics pavements once inside the Roman town Melita now forms part of Rabat as the Museum of Roman Antiquites.

In the Roman era the Melita area was enriched with palaces and temples, relics of which are the inscriptions, columns, capitals and mosaics in the Museum of Roman Antiquities.

The Rabat area is intimitaly connected with the introduction of Christianity in our islands: in A.D. 60 St Paul the Apostle, under arrest on his way to Rome and shipwrecked on our shores, is said to have lived our slept for three months in a cave within the ditch outside the walls of the old Roman city — St Paul's Grotto — and used it as a centre for his activity in establishing a primitive Christian community. This place has always been dedicated to St Paul — with an overstanding church and an important cemetery around it in the mediaeval period.

Burial being prohibited inside the walls of the city, the area outside the ditch, from St Paul's Grotto to Buskett, arounds with a concentration of hypogea — or burial places — of pagan, Jewish or Christian origin dug in live rock by the Phoenicians, Greeks, Romans and Byzantines. Their tombs contain a rich variety of architectural elements. The largest of these are the St Paul's and the St Agatha's complex in the Hal-Bajjada district.

Before the coming of the Knights Rabat became the centre of various religious Orders who preferred to erect their houses in a place not far from the capital city but also sufficiently secluded for their monastic recollection.

The Knights, centred on Vittoriosa and Valletta, erected very few constructions in Rabat and did little to embellish the area.

Today besides schools and colleges, Rabat has various social and band clubs, a market which is very popular on Sunday mornings, and playing fields. The Rabat area is ideal for walks in the countryside.

Museum of Roman Antiquities

The misnamed Roman "villa" Museum covers the site of a rich and sumptuously decorated town house belonging to a wealthy person in Roman Malta. The site, discovered in 1881 and further excavated in 1920-24, contains a number of remarkably fine mosaic polychrome pavements and some original architectural elements. A number of rooms were constructed to protect the mosaics and an upper hall was added to provide exhibition space and a suitable entrance. The porticoed neo-classical facade was completed in 1925.

Museum of St Paul's Church. The Collegio (Wignacourt College) was converted to a Museum in 1981. The access is either from the main door or else from an underground passage kewn in the rock in 1683 and linking the former residence of the officiating clergy with their church.

Below "St Paul by Francesco Zahra"

St. Agatha's church. Some photos of the Archaeological Museum which is housed in the same convent and crypt where we can admire the beautiful frescoes which are twenty-nine in all, go back to 1480 A.D. and are attribuited in majority to Salvatore d'Antonio

Mosta

Mosta is roughly in the geographical center of the Island of Malta and, in times gone by, it was considered to be far enough inland to be relatively safe from corsair attacks.

The chief attraction is now the monumental church which design was inspired by the Pantheon in Rome. Its dome is the fourth largest in Europe: the three other domes being in Rome, London, and Xewkija in Gozo. The building was started in 1833 and the church was consecrated in 1871; it was built around and over an older church which continued to be used during the time work was in progress. In the machine age in which we are living this sounds like an exceedingly long time, but one should bear in mind that the labour on this church was done on a voluntary basis, in the little spare time the people had at their disposal. This church, like many other of the older churches in Malta, could be said to be a monument of faith. In 1942 a thousand pound bomb penetrated the dome but failed to explode.

View of the large interior of Mosta church.

Comino

For long periods of its history Comino was an unsafe place in which to live, nevertheless, people did inhabit this tiny island on and off, the population figures fluctuating from nil to sparse.

In 1416 the Maltese petitioned the Aragonese king, Alphonse V, to build a tower on Comino as a deterrent to the corsairs who made it their base, but the people of the Island has to wait two hundred years before work was taken in hand; eventually the Tower of Comino was finished under Grand Master Alof de Wignacourt in 1618.

Despite the protection of the tower, people were chary of making Comino their home, in fact, the ancient church here, was desecrated in 1667 as being derelict; in 1716 the church was repaired and reconsecrated and, by this time the island had been repopulated to some extent.

With its handful of resident families and a single hotel, Comino, even now, has an air of a forsaken but beautiful island.

View of the small island of Cominotto seen from the splendid island of Comino situated between Malta and Gozo.

Gozo

Some years ago it was planned to connect the islands of Malta and Gozo by a bridge and Japanese engineers were called in to carry out a feasibility study. The project was considered technically possible but as the expense involved would have been considerable the plan was shelved. And many people in Malta, and many more in Gozo breathed a sigh of relief.

Should the Island of Gozo become too accessible there is a real danger of the island losing the old-word charm which Gozo has so far retained, and which Malta possessed and, unfortunately, lost some half century ago. The sister island of Malta is different from the larger island in that it is more fertile, more picturesque, and far more unspoilt; but what makes Gozo so markedly different from Malta are the Gozitans.

These frugal and tough people seem to be proof against any adversity, their character, like steel, has been tempered in the fire of privations and constant danger and they, and their descendants, have come out as better men from their ordeal.

Malta and Gozo share the same history and historical remains are duplicated in both islands, but Gozo has had more than its share of misfortunes. Largely undefended, the island has been many times devastated by piratical attacks and on one occasion almost the whole of the population was carried away into slavery.

When Gozitans had advance warning of an impending invasion, such as that of the Great Siege, some of them sought refuge in the better fortified towns of Malta and some of the old people were evacuated to Sicily, but as soon as it was safe for them to do so, they always returned home; Gozitans ransomed from slavery also returned home, it never entered their minds to settle in a safer place; Gozitan emigrants who strike it rich in the countries of their adoption likewise return home and build showy houses for themselves as evidence of their success. Perhaps what makes Gozo what it is, is the love and quiet pride of its inhabitants for their homeland. This pride is reflected, among other things, in the size and beauty of their churches.

Until a friendship is established, a Gozitan might be reticent, but once you make a Gozitan friend, you will have made a friend for life. The citadel in Victoria is a museum in itself, it is here that the rich Medieval families of Gozo had their own quarters in which to spend the night. In the esplanade below, in the square known as it-Tokk, one can see the more colourful side of Gozo. In the open market and in the souvenir shops around it are exposed for sale such local handicrafts as crocheted woollen dresses, the wool spun from the local sheep and the dresses worked by the island's women, as is also the famous Gozo Lace, a traditional, but still a very much flourishing, art.

Even if the Malta-Gozo bridge has not been built, communication between the islands is easy and frequent as car-ferries, hover-craft and yachts crisscross the six kilometre wide Gozo Channel.

May the increasing hordes of visitors to that island do not spoil its character and turn it into a smaller Malta.

The Cathedral (Below) designed by the Maltese architect Lorenzo Gafa in the form of a Latin cross was built between 1697 and 1711 on the site of an older church.

Archaelogical Museum. All archaelogical material found in Gozo is now shown in this 17th century house known as Casa Bondi. Of special interest are sherds of the Ghar Dalam phase (5000 B.C.) found at Ghajn Abdul, probably the oldest ever found in the Maltese islands and Majmuna tombstone, a beautiful marble inscription in Kufic characters dating to 1174 A.D.

St. George's Church

St. George's Church - St. George's Parish covers almost half of Victoria. This church was built in the 1670's and suffered severe damages in the earthquake of 1693. A new facade was built in 1818. The dome and the aisles are of recent construction.

There are many works of art in this church which include the paintings of the dome and ceiling by Gian Battista Conti of Rome and other paintings by Giuseppe Cali, Stefano Erardi and Mattia Preti. The beautiful statue of St. George was carved out of a trunk of a tree by Paolo Azzopardi in 1841.

The area over which the church is built of considerable archaelogical interest dating at least to the Roman period.

MVTAVIT ✠

It-Tokk, was the centre and probably, the market place as it is now.

In the side streets round the square one can by the delicious Gozo nougat, the "bankuncini" (almond based cakes) and the "pasti tassalib" which are Gozo's sweet specialities.

Xlendi. Is another summer resort used by the locals and tourists alike. In 1961 two shipwrecks dating about 2nd century B.C. and 5th A.D. were located on the sea-bed at the mouth of Xlendi Creek under 35 metres of water. Many amphorae and several lead anchor stocks have been recovered from these wrecks and are now at the Gozo Museum of Archaeology.

Dwejra - Dwejra is an area of outstanding natural beauty on the north-western coast of Gozo. It has been an attraction to the visitor for many centuries and we have representations of the Fungus Rock on many old engravings. The area in itself is a museum of history, archaeology, natural history and geology.

Inland Sea - The Gozitans call it "Il-Qawra". It is a sea-filled dissolution basin surrounded partly by the high cliffs and partly by a pebbly beach. The sea comes through a natural tunnel in the cliffs creating a big pool of clear sea water. The sea here is warmer and excellent for swimming especially for children. It gets deeper as one nears the tunnel.

THE ZERKA WINDOW (photo below)
This is massive natural archway cropping out of the sea.

Ta' Pinu Sanctuary

This is a national shrine and a centre of pilgrimages for both the Gozitans and the Maltese. On the spot there was a 16th century chapel dedicated to Our Lady of the Assumption with an altarpiece painted by Amedeo Perugino in 1619. On June 22nd 1883, Carmela Grima a middle aged peasant woman is reported to have heard the voice of Our Lady on this spot. This was followed by numerous acts of grace, miracles of hearling and Gozo escaping the plague the following year. Offering were sent to this chapel from all over the Maltese Islands as well as from abroad.

The present church was started in 1920 and consecrated in 1931. It was raised to the dignity of Basilica by Pope Pius IX a year later. The old chapel with the original painting can still be seen at the very end of the church where votive offering hang on either side of the shrine.

Built in the Romanesque manner, this church rises majestically on its own among the unspoilt Gozitan countryside surrounded by the hill of Ghammar and Gordan. It is a perfect example of workmanship and craftmanship in the Maltese stone. One notices the many intricate and different designs inside sculptured in the stone, and the mosaic pieces adorning the altarpieces and the frieze of the aisle.

A set of Carrara marble statues, lifesize, representing the Way of the Cross have been erected all along Ghammar Hill overlooking Ta' Pinu Sanctuary.

Marsalforn

This is the most popular summer seaside resort in Gozo. During summer, especially, the place is crowded with Gozitians, Maltese as well as tourists.

It started as a fishing village and the fishermen still keep their colourful boats in one sheltered corner of the Bay. Fresh fish is found in restaurant here throughout the years. During the hot months anyone can indulge in any king of aquatic sports. Bus transport to Victoria is in operation throughout the year at different times of the day, better still during summer. Marsalforn has a small sandy beach, several hotels, guesthouses, holiday flats, good restaurants, many souvenir shops offering any kind of Gozitan handicraft and other touristic amenities. Round the western headland are the coves of Qbajjar, Xwejni and the fjord-like cove of Wied il-Ghasri. On the eastern headland there are Ghar Qawqla, Ghajn Barrani and Ramla Bay.

Ġgantija Temples

The Ġgantija or, as it was commonly known in the past, "The Giants Tower", is the better preserved and by far the most impressive prehistoric temple. It is probably the finest of all ancient remains in these islands comparing with Stonehenge for grandeur. It was cleared round about 1826.

Ġgantija consists of two separate systems of courtyards which, like Mnajdra Temples, do not interconnect. They are known as the South Temple which is bigger, earlier (c. 3600 B.C.) and better preserved, incorporating five large apses and the North Temple which is smaller and a later addition (c. 3000 B.C.) in a 4-apse form. The great court of the South Temple measures 23 metres from apse to apse and the height of the wall here is preserved to eight metres, the highest in all the temples. Here one notices how the successive courses of stone draw in the manner of corbelling, though it is not possible that the aperture at the top was roofed with stones. The arch had not yet been known in building construction and the span of the apses here is quite large for any conceivable stone roofing. Wood or hides might originally have been used as roofing material.

Two kinds of stone had been used in the construction "tal-franka", the soft stone mainly used inside as portals and floor slabs, and "tal-qawwi", the hard stone which is mostly used for the general construction of the walls.

The interior of the walls was plastered and painted with red ochre. Traces of this have been found. The huge megaliths, forming the outer wall (the largest weighing several tons) were built alternatively, one horizontally and one upright. The space between the inner and outer walls is filled with rubble and earth. It is such a system which has given the Ġgantija the stability to withstand the depredations of over 5000 years. The floor is partly covered with soft stone slabs and partly with "torba", or beaten earth. Spiral and pitted designs decorate some of the soft stone slabs. Ore can hardly see the spirals today but considering their good state of preservation when the site was uncovered, this indicates that the temples had some kind of roofing protection during their use.

Ramla Bay

Ramla is a fine sandy beach on the north coast of Gozo, the best in both islands. Its name means "sandy". It is an excellent place for swimming and a great playing field for children.

On the next page: The small port of Mgarr with the recently built harbour, has always been Gozo's only link with the outside world.

© Copyright by Casa Editrice Plurigraf
S.S. Flaminia, km 90 - 05035 Narni - Terni - Italia
Tel. 0744 / 715946 - Fax 0744 / 722540 - (Italy country code: +39)
Tutti i diritti riservati. Riproduzione anche parziale vietata.
Stampa: 1995 - Plurigraf S.p.A. - Narni